A Lucky New Year

by Janet Stutley
illustrated by Shane Nagle

Table of Contents

Chapter 1
Red for Happiness

Ling and her family were getting ready for the Chinese New Year. It would be the Year of the Dragon. Ling knew that there were 12 animals in the Chinese calendar. Every year had an animal symbol.

Ling's father was painting their living room to welcome the New Year. At the same time, Ling helped her mother sweep out the kitchen and bedrooms. There was a lot of dust.

"Sweep out the old, sweep in the new," said her mother.

Ling went to the garden to fetch eight flowering branches. "Eight is lucky," she said.

Ling arranged the branches in a vase. The vase had a picture of a monkey, which is one animal in the Chinese calendar. Ling thought she saw the monkey look up at her. But it didn't move when she looked again. She thought her eyes were playing strange tricks on her.

"We will all wear our new clothes on New Year's Eve and New Year's Day," said her mother. "You can wear your red dress then."

"I'm glad that red is such good luck, because it's my favorite color!" said Ling.

"Is Cousin Ben coming over?" Ling asked.

"Yes, and your aunt and uncle. We'll go shopping tomorrow for our family dinner."

"I love going to the markets!" said Ling, as she spun around with joy.

"Careful, Ling, you know it's bad luck to break anything at this time," said her mother, who grabbed a huge bowl Ling had hit on the table. Ling turned around just in time to see what looked like a rabbit racing inside the bowl. That was another animal in the Chinese calendar!

"Sorry, Mom, but Chinese New Year is just the best time of the year!" said Ling, as she danced into the living room.

"Watch out!" her dad shouted. Some of the red paint spilled out of the can and onto the floor.

"Look!" said Ling. "The paint spilled out in the shape of a rat." It was another animal from the Chinese calendar. The rat looked up and winked at Ling. Ling's dad just shook his head at Ling. He didn't see anything.

Chapter 2
Food and Fireworks

It was the day of New Year's Eve.

"I've decided on the menu," said Ling's mom. "Let's go shopping."

They each took a large basket and walked through the busy streets to the market. Ling and her mom were headed for the fish stall. Ling knew her mother wanted to buy shrimp, oysters, and a fish for dinner.

At another stall, Ling's mom bought dumplings. "I have five dollars left," she said. "Do you want to get ice cream?"

Ling went to the ice-cream stall. She asked for a medium cup.

"That will be $3.50," said the man. Ling gave him the money and took the change.

"$1.50, I think that's the right money," she said to herself. Ling looked down at the stall and saw another animal on the Chinese calendar—a tiger. The painted animal nodded its head up and down, as if to say "It is!"

When they got home, Ling helped her mother cook. The dumplings simmered on the stove. Everything smelled wonderful.

Just before her relatives were due to arrive, Ling ran to change into her new red dress. Then she began to set the table.

Ling set three places. "That's half of the places. I think that's right," she judged. Then she set the other three places.

Next, Ling picked up a wall hanging of another Chinese calendar animal—a rooster. It also nodded its head to say she was right. This time Ling just smiled.

When her aunt, uncle, and cousin arrived, there was a lot of talking and laughter. It was a while before they were all assembled at the table. But then the food was devoured in a very short time.

"Mom!" said Ling. "You're forgetting about dessert!"

Ling's mom smiled. She brought out cakes and bright tangerines and oranges.

After dinner they played games. At midnight everyone went to the window to watch the fireworks. It was the start of New Year's Day!

🐉 Chapter 3 🐉
The Tray of Togetherness

The next morning, Ling's mom woke her up. "Ling, can you please fill the eight sections in the Tray of Togetherness for me?"

Ling's family was having more family visit for New Year's Day.

Ling bounced out of bed. "That's one of my favorite things to do!" she said. Then she heard a "baaa!" She was surprised, but she looked at her stuffed sheep. It was another Chinese calendar animal. Ling thought the sheep must be happy, too!

Ling took out the tray. She filled the first section with candied melon.

"That's one eighth," she said. In the next section she placed some red melon seeds. "That's one fourth done."

Then she filled two other sections with lychee nuts and cumquats. "That's half," she said. She filled the four sections that were left with coconut, peanuts, dried apricots, and lotus seeds.

Ling tried a little piece of sweet candied melon. Delicious!

"Can you bring me the ang pow packets, Ling?" her mom asked.

Ling picked them up. She loved getting her ang pow on New Year's Day. The packets bulged with a gift of money in them.

Ling looked at her bright red piggy bank. She dusted it off, and thought about the money she would be adding to it. The pig smiled. He enjoyed this time of year, too!

Her aunt and uncle arrived with her two cousins, Betty and Bobby. Everyone was dressed in his or her best clothes. The children were given their ang pow packets. Then they snacked from the Tray of Togetherness.

"Ling did all this while I was getting ready," said her mom, giving her a hug.

"Lucky for us, Ling has been a big help," said Ling's dad.

🐉 Chapter 4 🐉
Family Luck

Everyone was happy to go to the New Year's Day parade.

"Wait a minute," said Ling. She told her family that over the last few days she had seen seven animals in the Chinese calendar.

"I've seen the Monkey, Rabbit, Rat, Tiger, Rooster, Sheep, and Pig," said Ling. "That's seven. We need to see one more for good luck. Look for the Horse, Ox, Snake, Dog, or Dragon!"

When they got to the parade, Ling saw the Dragon. It was huge and red, and it twisted through the streets.

Dancers waved their arms and ran in and out of store doorways. Drums beat loudly. Ling's family looked happy together.

"Any day is a lucky day when you are with your family," the Dragon roared.

"Yes," said Ling. "We know we are very lucky!"

Comprehension Check

Retell the Story

Use a Fantasy and
Reality Chart and
the pictures to help
you retell this story.

Reality	Fantasy
What Could Happen?	What Could Not Happen?

Think and Compare

1. Turn to page 7. How did Ling know
   she got the right money from the
   ice-cream man? Explain how that shows
   fantasy or reality. *(Distinguish Between Fantasy and Reality)*

2. What would you enjoy most if you
   spent New Year's with Ling's family?
   Explain why. *(Apply)*

3. Why do families often get together
   on holidays? *(Analyze)*